MCL

Play Mas'! A Carnival ABC

DIRK McLEAN
ILLUSTRATED BY RAS STONE

TUNDRA BOOKS

To Renée, with love
To my Mas'-playing mother, Jacqueline
Special thanks to Kathy Lowinger and Mary Anne Cree
D.M.

To all of my children: Grow in Love
For all of life's blessings: Praise God
For all the people who touched my soul: Much Gratitude
R.S.

Text copyright © 2000 by Dirk McLean
Illustrations copyright © 2000 by Ras Stone

Published in Canada by Tundra Books, *McClelland & Stewart Young Readers*,
481 University Avenue, Toronto, Ontario M5G 2E9

Published in the United States by Tundra Books of Northern New York,
P.O. Box 1030, Plattsburgh, New York 12901

Library of Congress Catalog Number: 99-75643

Canadian Cataloguing in Publication Data

McLean, Dirk, 1956-
    Play mas'! : a carnival ABC

ISBN 0-88776-486-X

1. English language – Alphabet – Juvenile literature. 2. Carnival – Caribbean Area –
Pictorial works – Juvenile literature. I. Stone, Ras. II. Title.

PE1155.M535 2000   j421'.1   C99-932191-9

We acknowledge the support of the Canada Council for the Arts
and the Ontario Arts Council for our publishing program.

We acknowledge the financial support of the Government of Canada through
the Book Publishing Industry Development Program for our publishing activities.

Canadä

Design by Terri-Anne Fong

Printed and bound in Hong Kong, China

1 2 3 4 5 6   05 04 03 02 01 00

Play Mas'!

Between North America and South America lies the region of the Caribbean Islands, surrounded by the blue Caribbean Sea. There are three seasons here: Rainy Season, Dry Season, and CARNIVAL SEASON!

The Carnivals of the Caribbean are rooted in the French tradition of the Masquerade (Mas') and flavored predominantly by African and Spanish culture. They are generally a one-day, two-day, or week-long celebration. However, festivities begin weeks before.

Traditionally, Carnival takes place during the two days before Ash Wednesday and the beginning of the season of Lent. However, several islands have their Carnival at different times throughout the year. As a result, many people Carnival-hop; they go from one Carnival to the next and to the next. Imagine the fun!

Carnival is a time of freeing the body and the spirit – a time when one's worries, problems, and hardships are thrown aside – a joyous celebration of life. Think of it as the best party you can ever experience: see colorful dazzling costumes, dance in the streets, sing songs, hear music that makes your heart beat faster, reunite with friends you haven't seen in a long time, enjoy all of your favorite food and drinks, feel safe and protected, glow in the hot sun and let it energize you, join the competition for the best individual costume, and be in the best costume band.

Afterwards, you feel vibrant, renewed. Life goes back to normal. Until the next "party," until the next Carnival Season.

The influences of the West Indian style of Carnival can be seen outside the Caribbean on an annual basis in London (Nottinghill), England; in Brooklyn, Boston, and Miami in the United States; in Toronto, Winnipeg, Ottawa, and Montreal in Canada. As one Carnival ends, plans for the next one begin.

So, come, turn the pages, and see what Caribbean Carnival is all about.

Enjoy yourself and Play Mas'!

Dirk McLean

 Alonzo arranges art for Mas' Bandleader's approval.

 Braids, beads, and bamboo shake up in the Butterfly Band.

Celebrate colorful Carnival and Crop Over with cool coconut water.

 Dragon Mas' at Dimanche Gras dances into the night.

Everybody everywhere enjoys delicious edibles.

 Flagwoman leads the float past frying flying fish.

 "Get Something and Wave!" we sing in the Grandstand.

 Hold your headpiece high in the hot sun.

Imagine you are the Iron Man, setting irie rhythm.

 Jab Molassi jump up J'ouvert morning before the judges.

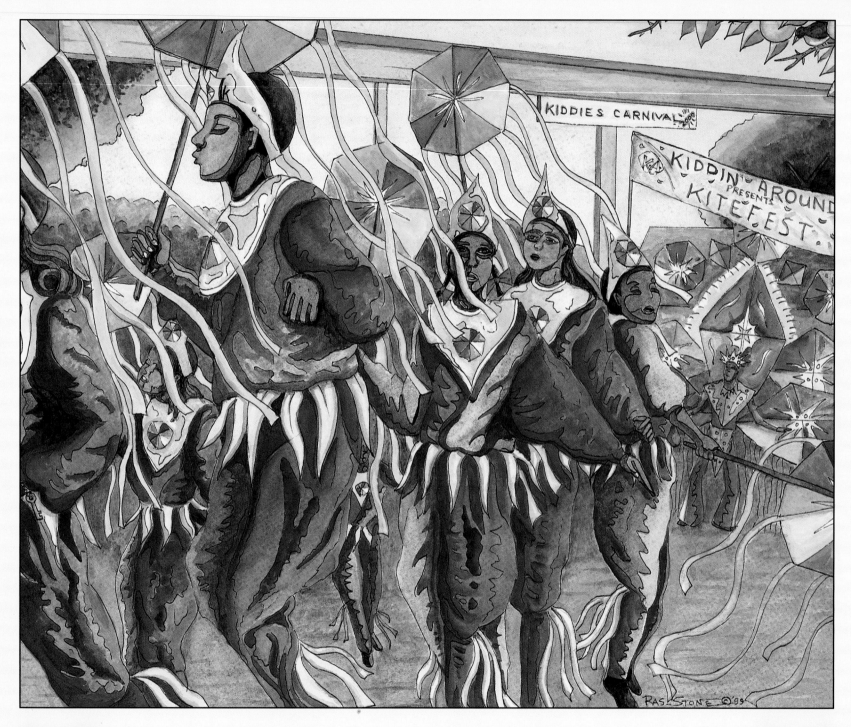

 Kiskidee sings in the king orange tree for Kiddies Carnival.

 Las' lap! We linger and limbo under the light of the moon.

 Make up the face and marvel at the merry Mas'.

 Now we don our neckpieces under a nutmeg tree.

Oysterman, Oysterman, observe all the Ol' Mas'.

 Panmen and Panwomen play in Panorama contest.

 The Queen of the Band wears quetzal feathers to compete.

 Rest for rice 'n peas and roti while the Roots Man fixes rainbow mask.

 See the steel drums scorched and shaped to satisfaction.

Try your talents in Calypso and Soca Tents.

 Ultrasonic sounds from the music trucks wind under our umbrellas.

 Victory-in-Europe Day. Our village's steel band takes to the streets.

 We watch the Wire-bender work with whorls of wire.

Dance in true-true Xante style.

Youthful sailors from the yachts join us every year.

 Zigzag steps and zebra stripes celebrate Zulu Mas'.

A Most costume Bandleaders decide on the theme for their Mas', then hire artists to sketch the costumes. Once the designs are approved, materials are purchased and the costumes made. From the sketches, people decide what section of the band they wish to play in.

B The word *band* in Carnival refers to a group of costumed masqueraders in different sections. Many bands have loyal players who provide the Leaders with repeat business every year. Bands often use beads – sewn onto costumes and braided into hair.

C Carnival Season involves calypso and soca singing (satirical songs, social and political commentary), the playing of steel drums, and the competition of bands. Tourists arrive from all over the world just for a taste of the festivities.

D Dimanche Gras is a competition that takes place on the Sunday evening before Carnival officially starts. Bands compete with their largest King, Queen, and Individual costumes for grand prizes.

E The eating of a variety of mouthwatering foods is a favorite pastime during Carnival. However, the food eaten is quickly danced off, leaving the masquerader hungry again.

F Flagwoman leads a steel band by dancing and waving a large flag with strength and great flair. Sometimes, only sometimes, the flag is waved by a man.

G The Grandstand, or main Carnival stadium seating, is the chief place where spectators watch the bands parade and compete. A skilled singer can move the crowd into a state of ecstasy.

H Headpieces vary more than any other article of a costume. They are usually easy to spot from a distance, or from behind high walls.

I Iron Men beat car tire irons with thin metal rods. They are key in setting and maintaining the rhythm for a steel band. This sound can be heard distinctly, although it often blends with that of the steel pans.

J J'ouvert (the opening celebration) begins just before dawn on the first Carnival morning. Masqueraders oil their bodies and apply white or brown mud, adding different colors of paint.

K Kiddies Carnival is also formally known as Children's Carnival. It is held through the streets, or through a stadium. Although there is adult supervision from the sidelines, these bands contain only children – of all ages. As long as the children have started to walk, they will dance at Carnival.

L Las' lap takes place on the final evening of Carnival. Masqueraders and spectators join together for a last dance through the streets before Carnival is officially over for the year, at midnight.

M Traditionally, the faces of the masqueraders were covered by masks. Today, the faces are mainly uncovered, and painted with many colors and designs. Carnival is affectionately known as Mas' – the time when people "Play Mas'."

N Costume accessories always include designed neckpieces, which vary in size and help to draw attention to the face.

O Ol' Mas' (Old Mas') shows historical costumes and figures of days gone by.

P Panorama is the competition to choose the best-playing steel band. The bands are made up of both men and women who practice for a long time, often learning the notes without using sheet music. They "beat the pans" with sticks that have a strip of rolled rubber on the tips.

Q One of the most dazzling and anticipated visions is that of the Queen of each band in competition at Dimanche Gras. Their costumes are huge and require painstaking hours to complete by true artisans; they are worth the labor.

R When the sun hits the costumes they become radiant. The costumes tell stories of the people and of the rebirth of their varied life experiences – from ordinary women's chores, like washing clothes by the river, to spiritual and historical reenactments.

S Steel drums were invented in the late 1930s, but even in the early 1940s they were considered a noise hazard and not allowed onto the streets. The steel pans begin as oil drums. They are cut to varying sizes; the tenor pan is the smallest and the bass is the largest, requiring the least cutting. They are tuned by a process of pounding the notes with a hammer and being heated over an open fire. It has been said that steel drums are the only musical instrument invented in the twentieth century.

T In the Calypso Tents the calypsonians, beginners and seasoned singers, practice and refine their calypsos and soca (soul-calypso) songs before audiences. This leads up to the Calypso and Soca Monarch Competitions at Dimanche Gras. The most popular songs are played by music bands on the road during Carnival.

U Apart from the music played by steel bands on the road, most music is played on top of huge long trucks, "big trucks." It can be heard blocks away.

V Victory-in-Europe Day (the day World War II ended in Europe) was Tuesday, May 8th, 1945 – the first day in Trinidad that steel bands were allowed onto the streets. People celebrated with wild jubilation to this new sound, which was finally accepted by the authorities.

W Wire-bending is a crucial step in the creation of the big costumes and floats. The wire is bent and sculpted, then covered with fabric or papier-mâché or any kind of paper. This skill is passed down. Once accomplished, the artisan becomes in great demand.

X The dancing at Carnival is very much a freeing of the body, allowing the participants to enjoy themselves completely.

Y An old saying tells us that you can't play Sailor Mas' and be afraid of the baby powder thrown on you. Powder floating in the air above the heads of the masqueraders creates a picturesque, dreamy sight.

Z Although Africans came to the Caribbean primarily from the west coast countries like Sierra Leone, Ghana, and Nigeria, quite a number came from South Africa. An inspired portrayal of Mas' is of the historic Zulu tribal costumes and dance.

Search each illustration for the following words. See how many you can find. Then, look for the hidden letter in each painting.

Aa apple, aloe plant, Arawak Studio, akee, airplane, artist, apron, ambulance, Africa clock, avocado

Bb boy, basket, bamboo, balloons, bongo drum, blue, black, bag, binoculars, bird, braids, bandannas, bottle, beads, buttons, Butterfly costume, banana leaf

Cc coconut, corn, car, camera, coal pot, caps, cutlass, coconut tree, cash

Dd dog, drum (talking), doves, dreadlocks, Dragon Mas', doll

Ee eggs, elephant headpiece, earrings, elbows, eyes, ears, evening, eyebrow, egg roll, ebony choker, eating, Earth Globe standards (wooden poles)

Ff feathers, flat hill, feeding, fingers, flags, fence, five dollars, foot, flamingos, fire, faces, float, Fancy Sailor (costume), flying fish, Flagwoman, flambeaux, flower

Gg guitar, gate, G-P (row), golf shirt, girl, glass, gray, green, glasses

Hh hat, hill, hands, hummingbird, hibiscus, hammock, headpieces

Ii iguana, iceman, iron, index finger, irie, infant, ID bracelet, ice-cream cone, Indian Mas', Individual of the Year (costume)

Jj juveniles, jetty, Jailbird (costume), Judge's Booth, Jab Jab (costume), Jab Molassi (costume), jumbie headpieces

Kk kites, kiskidee, king orange tree, knuckles, King of Carnival (Junior), Kiddies Carnival, key

Ll leaves, lizard, lemon tree, limestone, lagoon, log fire, limb, limbo dance, limbo sticks, lighthouse

Mm mangoes, mountain, morocoy (turtle), mouth, mask, mustache, Moco Jumbie (costume), Mas' (Masquerade) face, maxi taxi

Nn nose, necklace, nutmeg, nylon cape, nest, nuts, nut vendor

Oo orange, Oysterman, oysters, openmouthed, outfit, oil drum, owl

Pp parrot, palm tree, plumes, plantain leaf, purple, position, paper, pommerac tree

Qq Queen of the Band, quilted vest, Quarry Street, quick snap (camera), quetzal feathers, quarter to five

Rr radio, rainbow, river, roll of wire, ribbons, red, rose, roti, ruler, rock, rice 'n peas, Rastaman, roll of canvas, road, rooftops

Ss shirt, shoe, slipper, sticks, sour sop (fruit), spider, spiderweb, sailboat, ship, sugarcane, sun visor, straw hat, sno-cone, sandals

Tt trombone, trumpet, tamarind, truck, TV camera, tie-dye, trap, trinity hills

Uu umbrellas, uniform, unicorn, unicycle, under, upon

Vv vendor, vegetables, vines, vampire bat, valley, village, violets, vest, van

Ww wire, writing, whistle, watermelon, wallet, water, wick, watch, wrist, window, wall, wooden table, woman writing

Xx Xante dance, x's

Yy yellow, yardstick, youth, yacht

Zz Zulu, zip, zigzag, zebra stripes, zero, zaboca (avocado)